Macbeth in Venice

ALSO BY WILLIAM LOGAN

ଚଚ

POETRY

Sad-faced Men (1982)

Difficulty (1985)

Sullen Weedy Lakes (1988)

Vain Empires (1998)

Night Battle (1999)

CRITICISM

All the Rage (1998)

Reputations of the Tongue (1999)

Desperate Measures (2002)

Macbeth in Venice

WILLIAM LOGAN

PENGUIN POETS

PENGUIN BOOKS
Published by the Penguin Group
Penguin Group (USA) Inc., 375 Hudson Street, New York, New York 10014, U.S.A.
Penguin Books Ltd, 80 Strand, London WC2R 0RL, England
Penguin Books Australia Ltd, 250 Camberwell Road, Camberwell, Victoria 3124, Australia
Penguin Books Canada Ltd, 10 Alcorn Avenue, Toronto, Ontario, Canada M4V 3B2
Penguin Books India (P) Ltd, 11 Community Centre, Panchsheel Park, New Delhi – 110 017, India
Penguin Books (N.Z.) Ltd, Cnr Rosedale and Airborne Roads, Albany, Auckland, New Zealand
Penguin Books (South Africa) (Pty) Ltd, 24 Sturdee Avenue, Rosebank, Johannesburg 2196, South Africa

Penguin Books Ltd, Registered Offices:
80 Strand, London WC2R 0RL, England

First published in Penguin Books 2003

10   9   8   7   6   5   4   3   2   1

Page xi constitutes an extension of this copyright page.

LIBRARY OF CONGRESS CATALOGING-IN-PUBLICATION DATA
Logan, William, 1950
   Macbeth in Venice / William Logan.
   p. cm.
   ISBN 0-14-200302-6
   1. Venice (Italy)—Poetry. 2. Punchinello (Fictitious character)—Poetry. 3. Macbeth, King of Scotland,
   11th cent.—Poetry. I. Title.
PS3562.O449M33 2003
811'.54—dc21   2002045030

Printed in the United States of America
Set in PoliphilusMT with BladoMT Italic & Designed by Sabrina Bowers

 *for Debora Greger*

∞ Contents

∞ The Shorter Aeneid

∞ Punchinello in Chains

&c; Venetian Hours

&c; Macbeth in Venice

❧ Acknowledgments

The *Antioch Review:* Gli Insetti di Venezia

The *Kenyon Review:* Ca' d'Oro

The *Nation:* Leaving Venice

New England Review: Marco Polo among the Insects, Torcello

The *New Republic:* The Lost Birds of Venice

The *New Yorker:* The Saint and the Crab

Notre Dame Review: Canova at the Fish Market

The *Paris Review:* The Quicksand Builders,
  The Shorter Aeneid

Poetry: Macbeth in Venice

Sewanee Theological Review: The Massacre of the Holy Innocents

The *Sewanee Review:* Punchinello in Chains

Southwest Review: The Church of San Fantin

Not every one that brings from beyond seas a new gin, or other jaunty device, is therefore a philosopher.

—*Thomas Hobbes*

Macbeth in Venice

The Shorter Aeneid

I. ☙ *The Ship*

"The Fighting Temeraire,"
—*J. M. W. Turner*

The sunlight burned like wire on the water
that morning the ghost ship drove upriver.
The only witness was a Jersey cow.

Florid and testy, a miniature industrialist,
the steam tug spouted its fiery plume of smoke,
and on the bank the dead trout lolled,

beyond the reach of fishermen now.
From a distance the fish lay sprawled like sailors
after a great sea battle, the masts and spars

splintered like matchsticks on the water, the mist
hovering over inlets, cannon smoke drifting
off the now purple, now green bloom of river.

In shadow a train inched a brick viaduct
ruling the still-dark valley,
as aqueducts once bullied the dawn campagna.

The cows resented the Cincinnatus patriot,
knowing they were bred for slaughter.
The morning was a painting: the battered warship

hung with dawn lights like a chestful of medals,
the barren canvas of the Thames, empty out of respect,
the steam tug beetling to the breaker's yard.

The sun lay on the horizon like a vegetable.

3

II. ∞ *The Train*

The medieval green of brackish hedge
took the window of the train like tapestry.
Hawthorns bristled the jigsawed spines of map,

broken like the millefleurs duchies of Europe.
How long had they fallen on discontented earth,
travelers twisting their watches to catch the light?

From darkness to darkness, across the ragged
carte du pays, folded in your lap were headlines,
and as I slept in my tarnished suit

the decade vanished and we were strangers again.
None of the new-risen worlds had fallen.
Then I awoke, and you *were* gone, nothing on your seat

but the unread *Times.* I looked out the window
as we shunted through dressed-up, derelict stations,
past a dirt track climbing a humpbacked ridge,

fields of crooked poppies an Impressionist blur,
and you swayed into the aisle
as we crossed a burnt-out farm.

Behind us lay the ruined city,
a Rome of chimneys the stalks of blown weeds.
Your hair caught something flashing

at the curtain fall of evening.

III. ❧ *Refugees*

LONDON, 1945

Two ravens flared across the blue-edged field,
political evening lit by veins of flint
as if each spark struck a single word

as night opened a ploughed dictionary.
On the bomb-scarred platform, we stood
beside our cardboard cases, the crowd milling

like gray, intolerant ghosts. We passed
into the city as clocks chimed the wounded hour.
Evening, the time between two worlds,

shivered down the naked barometer.
The gas streetlamps glowed like mercury
and over the chimneys of cobbled walks

martins like Spitfires darted through clouds
of insects. Each brick house a sooty curtain
above a sprocketed bay. Odor of smoke and bacon fat.

Beneath iron gutters, birds beat back their wings
and fluttered to clamorous nests, each bearded nest
a mouth that served no native tongue.

You leaned against me on the hollow street.
We had entered that wasp-waisted country
with paper tags pinned to our wool coats,

only our passports insisting where we belonged.

IV. ॐ *The Oracle of the Birds*

What shelters the arms of exile, the oracle asked,
the shield of the mute or shell of the deaf?
Under the crossed necks of swans

that burn but cannot speak, the rage of words
batters the brass gates of the throat.
Even one word may be a Trojan horse,

each damascened letter a drawn sword.
Words flower on the pool of the dead—
even a letter knows revelation in a threat,

revolution in a thread.
From the soil of crumbling London come,
as if through that other world,

the marble fragments of Augustan Rome,
each letter chiseled to the slow-motion of empire.
Speak, there was never time to speak

beneath the muffled engines of eternity.
Silence, there will be time for silence,
to be buried with the words unspoken,

your mouth stopped with cemetery gravel.
They invite the purchase of history, icy in its ellipses,
its freeze-dried gallery of moments,

momentum in equal fear of past or future.

V. ❦ The Other World

In Venice, once, I beheld that other world,
the prewar rooms of water,
lights of decaying palazzi floating

ghostlike, eerie as fish, in the drowned canals.
The opera house guttered like a candle,
and through its open windows

glared an almost-sky almost innocent.
That black morning history was unmade elsewhere,
I stood uncertain of my path,

"staked-out," as you say, by a lounging Englishman
beneath the hotel's rusted sign,
a tiny compass in his cupped palm:

"Aeneas, throw away your canvas map.
Here on the back canals, the houses lull
on limestone rotted by retreating tides,

the pleasure of palazzi on the mud,
the crossed wake of the gondolas, oaring past
to songs their fathers' fathers sang to tourists,

though finally none are tourists here. Each night,
the singer's little gasp and clutch of pain
float to the upper windows, like an aria—

the mud below still casts the doge's bones.

VI. ∞ *The Other World*

"I'll guide you through a labyrinth of names
you would not recognize, insistent ghosts
lost to the city of glass, city of water,

where the Rialto's history is engraved
within the cheeselike mortar of the stone,
each choked canal a circle of the dead.

You cannot see the starving corpses stand
up to their necks amid the pea-green sewage,
their toes like snails upon the leathery slime.

Tourists are rowed among them as if blind.
The six-toed cats can see, see the old doge
hauled on his barge, his gilded trumpets roaring,

the painted sailcloths taut against the breeze,
his sails the flayed skins of his enemies.
He judders across a bay of flailing arms

that plead for pardon in the burning waves.
Each watery vesper they sink beneath the waves,
invisible to all the chittering crowd,

to all except the quayside's Moorish cats.
On tiptoe in his handmade suit, the doge
scatters his blessings and indulgences,

the black confetti of his government.

VII. &c. *The Other World*

"Our air is stained in phosphorescent burning,
the glare of Mestre's factories alight,
the blaze of gas across the storage tanks

on midnight's dreaming skin, the sugary poisons
in the draining stones, where cold acids tear
holes in the veins of marble, and carbons ink

tattoos upon the forearms of the gods.
Beneath these gods I stole a *nom de guerre,*
ever to wave my diplomatic passport

across the borders of the other world.
I told the empire from the emperor,
who pensioned me upon hexameters

to script the gods their VC's in the war.
The empress bore an India on her crown
and Africa adorned her swanlike neck.

America graced her second-best tiara.
My soul debates the world in a hearing aid.
On starless nights the dead men strut

backward along the course of filled canals,
their heads above the pavement, moaning, moaning
their bargain grievances and antique pain.

They rate two stars within your Baedeker.

VIII. ✣ *The Other World*

"Due north the jagged street of traitors lies,
where men rip out their tongues, and there we cross
the alley of assassins, where the stones have eyes.

Jam your fist into the politicians' drain,
plugged with the guts of fish. Behind this wall,
in bricked⁄up campos where a plane tree grows,

the old ones breakfast on their common prayers.
The two ghosts you have asked for cannot speak.
The woman turns her face away and laughs.

The blind man counts his rosary of debt
beside the Grand Canal. Most of the dead
have nothing left to say to those alive.

Last you must mark the campo of Marco Polo,
who watched the godlike khan amid his tents,
who walked the trackless waste, knew burning gods,

saw catwalks in Milan and Rome, an F⁄16
writing its landlocked battles on the air,
the boiling ruby of the laser beam,

who after decades lying among the living
returned to this archipelago of lies.
Some say he never left Albania.

Some say his China was just poetry.

IX. ❧ *The Other World*

"Within these garden walls, a Persian cat
descended from the sacred cats of Rome
gave Eve the fish of wisdom and our sins.

Venice rewrote the book of Genesis:
the waters of the Flood belch from these drains;
the dove of Noah spies, atop the ocean's slur,

the Campanile hoisting its angel like a buoy.
The rushes of that barren islet thieve
the orphan Moses for the doge's arms,

the *acqua alta* dividing at his hand
to drown the Austrian privates as they sleep.
Where Cain slays Abel on San Marco's steps,

beneath the horses of Apocalypse,
the blood-stained *pavimenti* heave and split.
Now Joseph's polychrome bathrobe is on sale

behind the plate glass of Missoni's shop;
and off the street of arrowmakers stands
the temple of American Express,

where each lost soul redeems his ancient pledge.
Each church a Calvary, each black canal a hell."
Then my stooped guide, muttering of emperors,

walked through Fortuny's silks and disappeared.

X. ✸ *The Book of Genesis*

Where doges reigned, young Taglioni danced,
and Ruskin practiced Byron's halting step
while Henry James declaimed in the voice of God.

Bright with a vat of foam, like God he worked,
covering the floor as if with an ocean of surf,
the Venetian come to scrub the Turkish carpets.

Breathing like a sirocco, as if the eighth day
could scour the old world clean again,
he passed his hand over the darkness of the kilim,

the hum of his machine a fatal tide.
No ark this time with its quarrelsome crew,
no pairs of animals, predator locked up with prey,

nothing within the devil's rage of temptation,
nothing that might go wrong in the aftermath.
I saw on him the thing I came to see

each morning thereafter on myself, the face of evil.
Brow furrowed like a water-god's, the Venetian was gone,
sweating and overweight, his tie crooked,

still like a god, though old like a god,
as if he had known all this before.
His brushes were worn down to stubs—

he suffered along with the cleaning.

XI. &@ *The Book of the Lizard*

Night. The color of battle. Written across the moon,
a lizard took a burning moth in its mouth.
You lay across Procrustes' bed,

beneath the cotton disarrangement of sheets.
The words you took into your mouth
lost the fate of words. That night in Venice,

you stood within the charred conch of La Fenice.
Sunday morning, in dawn's bright order,
the church we entered was a cold, dangerous world,

its shedding plaster walls a map
of the unknown: fallen worlds, here and there
revealing the filthy lath all worlds are plastered on.

You could not find your way back,
back to the gold boat hammered thin
with its threadlike gold oars; back to the mosaic boat

mortared to the ceiling of San Marco,
the boat in which they smuggled the corpse of Mark
packed in a barrel of salt pork;

back to the rocking, dark *traghetto* that prowled
the waves at its decaying dock. The weather fair,
the distance across the water far, too far.

Words, words, naked as prey to predator.

XII. ∞ *Measure for Measure*

The ornamental plum frizzled into daylight,
dank, pinkish, slightly scorched blossoms
floating, alien as Byron's money

on the exchange boards of shuttered banks.
They fell in still life, snow in a woodblock print,
dappling the mottled carp in kept ponds.

The plum married the plum of another country
above the dead empire of ferns,
their curled skeletons a row of bishop's croziers.

Unseasoned cold, searing as summer heat,
had borne away the surface of the garden,
each wart and fissure apprentice to the new world.

Three days of cold, and Christ's roses would not rise again,
taken from the life, in the old phrase.
The lost house was cold, cold in the guarded spring,

Queen Anne's lace laced up in Queen Anne's style.
You burned in the surfaces,
and beneath green water a face peered up at me.

What is timeless, the glebe cow or the monument?
Already fiddleheads uncurled above the waste
and termites sang like dryads in the wood.

The garden had to be rebuilt like a city.

Punchinello in Chains

I. ∞ *Punchinello Hatched by a Turkey*

Above the egg, a turkey spread its wing
to warm the malformed contents of the thing.

The mules and stabled cattle now stood still
to bless the Incarnation of the Will.

The egg, as heavy as a man could hold,
rocked on the hay nest like a miniature world.

The turkey cock's coarse cries, like weeping cellos,
jostled the hats of humpbacked Punchinellos,

and twelve disciples leaned against the nest
as the pale sunlight moldered in the west.

A tin star burned in the hayloft—angels stirred,
and so commenced the Triumph of the Word.

A rapping rap. A groan of a groan. They watched
the eggshell crack—and Punchinello hatched!

II. ❧ Punchinello in the Menagerie

PUNCHINELLO INTRODUCED TO SOCIETY
BY THE OSTRICH

They've come by night to watch the ostrich strut,
these ruffled ladies of the candled villa,
late hack work of the late Palladio
(the powdered buttresses, the fallen arch).
Young Punchinello takes its wings in hand
to measure out gavottes along the path.
The ostrich bows and breaks off their engagement.
What a fine sergeant it would make, feathers
beating against the legions of Napoleon,
whose storm clouds rise above the Alps. Venice,
what raises Venice if the mainland falls?
The ostrich prances, and castrati fall
in love or down the steps of our new play.
Ice‑blind canals have primed old cannonballs.

PUNCHINELLO CONFUTES THE DANCING DOGS

The dogs have closed their dance, the dancers flee,
barking down *calli,* across the iron bridge.
The bagpipe gasps for air, a tambourine
cracks its scraped skin, the older musics fall.
By night the shadows shift, playing across
an ancient hero on an ancient stone—
the bronze sword lifted up, or melted down,
has ransomed *condottieri* to their fates.
Low whispers flood dark corners with their plots,
and vanished arts fill wormy dressing rooms.
Now winter's icy lock has rusted shut.
The portrait of the old doge fades and cracks.
The world is living backwards, dying forwards—
a globe revolves in Punchinello's hands.

III. ❦ The Marriage of Punchinello

The bride's brocade hangs like a cerement.
Her black pearls stare—were they the eyes of squid?
Poor Punchinello does not know if love
can separate the ego from the id.

His thoughts drift from the ceremony's grave
sacrament to the wedding bed apart—
he wonders if a marriage of true minds
will soon betray the treason of the heart.

Above the scene, pale ladies of the stairs
loll in vain commerce for vague gentlemen
whose battered passions come at bargain prices.
They buy new vows with old napoleons.

In churches raised from the dust of ancient Rome,
each wooden Christ hangs gilded like a whore
and casts its painted eyes along the walls'
forgotten booty from forgotten war,

while Punchinello in his beak-nosed mask
faces the future with a rueful grin.
He knows that every mongrel has his day
and every Christian sacrament its sin.

IV. ∞ *Punchinello in Chains*

What have I done?, poor Punchinello said.
Constables bound him with an iron ring,
yanking his body from the bedbugged bed.
Outside the cardinals began to sing.

Constables bound him with an iron ring,
clanking and mocking down the narrow stairs.
Outside the cardinals began to sing.
The citizens returned to their affairs.

Clanking and mocking down the narrow stairs,
a whore held up her skirts in disbelief.
The citizens returned to their affairs.
Each new arrest had come as a relief.

A whore held up her skirts in disbelief—
mere sympathy could not release the clown.
Each new arrest had come as a relief.
There was no mercy in the shallow town.

Mere sympathy could not release the clown
who dragged Christ's cross around the flooded square.
There was no mercy in the shallow town,
whose black canals made mortal thoroughfares.

Who dragged Christ's cross around the flooded square?
Not I, said Punch, bowing his battered head,
whose black canals made mortal thoroughfares
silent among the mercies of the dead.

Not I, said Punch, bowing his battered head,
and prayed forgiveness for a life of sin
silent among the mercies of the dead.
No godless heaven wants to let you in.

"Who prayed forgiveness for a life of sin?"
said hungry priests in each cold house of God.
"No godless heaven wants to let you in.
Take mercy from the octopus and cod."

Said hungry priests in each cold house of God,
"No man still living knows how death will go.
Take mercy from the octopus and cod."
Loving each other will not make it so.

No man still living knows how death will go
yanking his body from the bedbugged bed.
Loving each other will not make it so.
What have I done?, poor Punchinello said.

V. &a. *The Trial of Punchinello*

His eye blown glass, his nose a wormy fig,
a magistrate shook the dead lice from his wig,
harumphed for quiet through the stifling court
(for some each guilty verdict was a sport),
and bawled for Punchinello's last appeal.
A bailiff glaring like a spitted eel
dragged shivering Punchinello to the dock.
The other magistrates glanced at the clock,
the shackles clinked, a duchess changed her seat,
outside the uproar roared up in the street.
A line of prisoners crouched like pinchbeck priests;
the flyblown clerics slouched like young artistes;
a half-blind painter grouched like a famous felon.
(Poor Punchinello's head felt like a melon,
or cantaloupe, perhaps—in any case some fruit
no Juris Doctor ever dared confute.)
Blind Justice is an abstract sort of girl
who in the ballroom gives an abstract whirl,
but in the courtroom voltas to a tune
where innocence in May is guilt in June.
She's not a girl you'd take home to your mother
(no girl is ever good enough for Mother):
a dirty handkerchief conceals her blindness;
the tarnished scales weigh out her least unkindness
to every misdemeaning rake or fellow
born to the honest name of Punchinello.
We know confession by what we confess
(and know possession by what we possess),
but in the dock poor Punchinello stood
as if this were an unknown neighborhood.
Behind the pasteboard mask, his guilty eyes
rose to the antic whirring of the flies,
to new-laid rivers staining antique plaster,

and cracks that spelled out some word like . . . *disaster.*
A chandelier descended on a rope,
each candle burning like a misanthrope,
as if each flicker were a signal flare
to warn the queen great Agamemnon's there.
Such bedtime stories, since the fall of Troy,
have stirred the rakish blood of every boy
against the cold soliloquies of treason—
or blinded him to passions of sweet reason.
Great tales of valor stir the hero's hope,
though heroes often end beneath the rope,
because for heroes there's no greater crime
than being too heroic for your time.
The jailer's clock is ever slow to bless
the prisoner's resistance to confess
the sins of love (or call them crimes of state)
committed by each lowly vertebrate—
poor tragic Love must find an iron cage
in which to write the memoir's dirty page.
Once Casanova stalked the Bridge of Sighs,
where grieving Innocence forgets her lies
and dewy Guilt recalls her swift consent
(except at Easter, Michaelmas, and Lent);
but Punch stood charged in capital degree
of murder's post-Nicene philosophy,
high treason's selfishness, dull bribery's doubt,
theft's disappointment, and low water's drought.
The lawyers jawed, the magistrates jawed back,
but Punch's clotted ears could not keep track.
As sensibility's the end of sense,
poor Punchinello dreamed of innocence,
the homely cottage with its homely door,
the welcome rat beneath the welcome floor,
the village church beneath the village steeple,
where simple plague kills off the simple people.
They lie at last, the coward and the brave,

within the narrow circuit of the grave.
The magistrates intoned a weary hour
about the state's religious gift of power,
the obligation of blind law to rule
the wayward king, the gondolier, the fool,
Fate's disenchantments and the Alpine snows,
the Lord's forgiveness and the doge's toes.
They criticized the old, rebuked the young,
then sentenced Punchinello to be hung.

VI. ✄ *Punchinello Dreams of Escape*

The ship at anchor wasn't what it seemed—
yet Punchinello gripped the eagle's neck.
(The dream of life is just another dream.)

It soared above the masts, canals, the steam
of chimneys, till our Punch was just a speck.
The ship at anchor wasn't what it seemed,

the harbor, Venice, Europe—even the gleam
blazing San Marco's horses shrank. A fleck!
The dream of life is just another dream

that really wants a king, a god's regime,
or some poor hurricane to wreck
the ship at anchor. Wasn't what it seemed,

Punch's old life, another Ponzi scheme?
Weren't sailors waving from the quarter-deck?
The dream of life is just another dream

that none of us will live to see redeemed.
Death scrawls his bold John Hancock on your check.
The ship at anchor wasn't what it seemed.
The dream of life is just another dream.

VII. ∞ *The Hanging of Punchinello*

The arms went slack, the crooked heart unstrung,
when Punchinello from the gallows hung.

An idea formed inside the knotted rope,
which seemed to stiffen slightly, then lost hope.

His eyes were bandaged by the handkerchief
a thief had taken from another thief.

The weeping of a girl. A muffled cough.
No passing breeze could shake the shackles off.

High on a dappled horse, the hangman swore,
waving his sword above a yapping cur.

Two ladders pointed toward a dusty heaven.
The vultures circled, waiting to get even.

Below the mountain pass, a postcard town.
The guilty man decided to come down.

VIII. ⬧ *The Resurrection of Punchinello*

Above the monuments and greasy tombs
the dusty larks sang ceaselessly of sex,
a patch of bushes claimed, twelve fiery blooms,
the doom that hung above their little necks.

Not three days in the ground, a hungry Punch
loitered along the path, eager to meet
his friends now making pilgrimage, or lunch,
among the graves on Cemetery Street.

They wanted nothing hot-blessed but the sun,
forgiveness of their sins, a wicked pun.
They took one look and saw oblivion—
poor Punchinello was a skeleton.

Venetian Hours

∞ The Quicksand Builders

The quicksand builders built
against the Folly of All.
They built from ancient custom.
They built for the good of the Wall.

As fast as they built, it sank,
and as fast as it sank, they built.
They felt no loss or sorrow,
no residue of guilt.

As long as they stayed on the job,
there was hope that the job would go.
The common people knelt
and prayed to the gods below.

The builders knew no gods
could save like a hard bed of silt,
and as fast as they built, it sank,
and as fast as it sank, they built.

‏ *The Lost Birds of Venice*

The hotel entrance was painted green—faux marble.
　Our rooms perched on a dead-end street
and backed on a dead canal.

　The walls were spotted as if with moldy roses.
Pigeons warred in arcs across the great piazza,
　scolding, in their ragged voices,

the four bronze chargers
　who peered down shyly, like carousel horses,
from the balcony of San Marco

　(a "warty bug out for a stroll," suggested Twain).
Where were the famous songbirds of Venice?
　Wing chairs perched in the echoing palazzo.

Gilt frames were crowded with gondolas,
　with preposterous mob-capped doges,
glass-cheeked pages and jealous senators,

　a swarm of minor bribed officials,
and, as an afterthought,
　nothing in the afterthought of sky.

A boy lounging in a gondola,
　slightly removed from the procession on Ascension Day,
bored, at ease with youth, with the mild

　unafflicted plunder of possibility,
without thought for the black-cloaked sailors,
　the quiet burial on one of the outer islands,

stared into the choppy lagoon,
    where the waves—wavelets, really—
were whited in like wood shavings. Inverted *v*'s!

    As if the lost birds of Venice
had tired of flying, flying forever,
    and plunged downward on the melted wings of Icarus,

glad that they must die.

✂ Marco Polo among the Insects

Like a water-strider, the dainty water-taxi
skitters the puckered skin of the lagoon,
tipsy gondoliers bellowing ripe insults
in its wake. Their faces glow like saints.

Where have our blasphemies gone sailing now?
There, into the Campiello del Squellini—
behind a midnight countess's flapping cape,
an emerald bug has fallen to the ground,

bright scarab lost to the flare of Mongol campfires.
Night drifting on the ice-bound steppes has sewn
a thousand beetles to her glittering dress.
And what new monster had Marco Polo seen,

limping back the broken coasts of India?
The water-soaked guidebook points our glassy eyes
to a Byzantine arch, swallowed like a wasp
inside the ripening fig of a later wall,

its blunt curve fingered out in weathered cranes,
drowsy lions with stubs of limestone paws
that sharpened their appetites on Marco Polo.
In time this insignificant courtyard was

renamed the Corte Prima del Milion,
the beetle-browed, well-armored citizens
believing his black dreams mere fairy tales.
They wore the carnival masks of living bugs.

✑ *Canova at the Fish Market*

Canova's marble pyramid—uneasy amid
    the rococo doges, each block a lesson in Euclid—
offers its jigsaw to the puzzle of the dead.

    There, the lamenting hooded ghost;
there, the ghost of marble draped on marble,
    as if their cold possession of the stone

had grown sad, mute, insupportable. Below
    the vaulting of the Frari, four monstrous African slaves
shoulder the heaving shelf of a doge's triumph,

    ebony skin splitting their marble trousers,
muscles bearing their world as wounds.
    A sniggering black skeleton staggers over all.

Where does the sculptor humble himself to stone?
    Fish-market capitals carved in outland figures
of seahorse, squid, or octopus, boats shored

    against the stone, Halloween creatures of the lagoon.
From what marble depths of water
    does salt eat the crevices of their pores?

Fish unnamed, unsalable, lie beneath the sweet
    vaginal stink of the market stalls, wooden tables
tilting their boxy metal trays—blue-veined

    steaks of tuna, ropy lengths of the sulking eel,
bullet-headed mullet, open-mouthed red gurnet,
    translucent bulb of the humble cuttlefish.

There, the bloated faces of drowned politicians,
    there, sailors of the bribery and the fraud
lament the salty nets of commerce.

∞ Gli Insetti di Venezia

Above the hissing jet of cold blue flame,
the glassblower draws a blot of ink-black glass
into the molten image of an ant.
It joins the chain of ants

winding across the Sahara on his bench.
His window swarms with purple beetles,
a stiffened flock of Monarch butterflies,
the clean athletic body of the mantis.

The Turkish warehouse
displays a necklace of dinosaur vertebrae
and the femur of a lizard Ozymandias
risen from the red sand of the Gobi.

The lies of evolution play to Lazarus:
creamy decaying fish upended in glass jars,
iridescent butterflies like broken mosaics,
bugs the merest scraps of marbled paper.

The Cretaceous horseshoe crab, marooned
on its isle of slate like a fossil Crusoe,
skittered from one broken floe to the next,
its feathery claw-prints faltering to a dead stop.

And there, pressed like a prom-night orchid
between the wafery leaves of mud
is the buried crab itself.
A robot mantis bows its head. *Mantide religiosa*.

The whining motor spreads its vicious forelegs.
as if to take the child who stands weeping before it.
The gears grind a little, the religious engine hums.
Sand unto sand, intones the Priest of Glass,

forgive us, O Lord, our Transparent Sins
and deliver us from the Shattering of Evil.
In the glassblower's window
lounges a little mantis family:

The Holy Ghost has a broken leg.
The Father seems to be devouring the Son.

✣ The Church of San Fantin

Plaster fell from the broken lath, like snow.
    The priest, a shroud of cuttlefish ink,
shuffled as if the world were black ice.

    The orange marble was spotted like plum cake.
Dipping the holy rag once, twice,
    into the font, he wiped the crooked floor,

empty waves that broke against the damned.
    What lay beneath the frozen stone,
beneath the translucence of the Pliocene?

    Souls of early saints, fossil shells
martyred for quiet sea-floor heresies,
    coarse-sawn to pave the sin of shelving slabs.

A wooden Christ, lowered from his wall, slept
    along the floor, cross tilted on an altar edge
blossoming with throats of Easter lilies.

    Outside, rain swept the campo like molten tin.
Low boats rocked against the painted swell.
    Draw rain's veil over your eyes, strangers,

bow your heads, as if the pre-recorded music
    were a choir of angels.
As if craftsmen were not gilding angels again.

    A lone barge chunkered by, loaded with soiled laundry.
We bowed to the adoration of the shells
    for whom death came too soon, all too soon.

৵ The Saint and the Crab

Along the campo, Manin's bronze winged lion prowled
among the tanned intruders, licking their hands.
Pools of iridescent shellfish
lay open in the restaurant window,

a shop of otherworldly opals, the mussels' sheen
the skies of a closed heaven, crabs flat on their backs,
their armor intricate trapped plates and escapements.
The squid slumped in its own ink, the octopus appalled

in its slime. Many and ingenious are the postures of death.
But look! There, in a corner, beneath a willowware plate,
a lone crab clicked its claws, creeping
over a casket of walleyed fish,

through a valley of oysters keeping their counsel,
only to shift warily under the shadow of a wine bottle.
Which saint, O saints, watches over the saintly crab?
The man of forks and spears, the man of arrows?

In the Ca' d'Oro, the stiffened Sebastian takes
each arrow through his flesh like a skewer.
He wears a little napkin around his middle.
Saint, watch over the fragile boat of the runaway crab.

Let him steal his way back to the green lagoon,
go floating down the Grand Canal on his own *motoscafo*.
Let him take second life, a later martyrdom.
Let him wave his bent claws in a mockery of farewell,

lest we eat in his hollow shell his captive meat.

The Massacre of the Holy Innocents

Venetian, 14th century

Even the guards had faces grizzled like stone.
    Within the cold shadows of the museum,
their silence reigned without agreement,

    light contracting to the windowpanes,
the pierced loggia hung with plastic film.
    Here the rotting palazzo, beam-ends

eaten down to nubs, floors puffy with age,
    floated on its perilous wooden raft,
pilings sunk deep into Venetian clay.

    The massacre rose against us like a mirror,
the stone torn and ragged,
    one soldier anchored to his shield,

hand gripping his pike like an athlete,
    but missing his head, another frog-marching
a woman cradling an amputated child in her arms.

    Other children had been reduced to stubs of feet.
One mother stared out blankly through granite—
    a mailed torso stood protecting her,

an act of kindness in our undiscovered country.
    A second look, a third.
The soldier, hideously maimed himself,

    had torn the stone baby from her arms.

🕮 Ca' d'Oro

Calm. Meditation. Across the Grand Canal,
the open fretwork winkles the noonday sun.

Where once the loggias were slipped with gold,
the praise of Ruskin fixed the modern line,

wringing his brushes on his laundered shirt.
Against the hot glass, even the flies recoil.

To see the old Ca' d'Oro in its plumage,
and not the rotted spars of the upper floors,

the Gothic stairway ripped out like a molar,
the eye must blind the chalky dim republic,

spun-sugar battlement and tracery,
the pierced facade glaring like broken eggshells,

between grace and history nothing but a will to power.
Beyond the swelter of the Turkish warehouse,

palazzi eat their owners like *buccelati.*
A summer squall trembles over the lagoon,

the church's wilted gray, arching in afterlight.
The canal boils to the pavement edge;

stalled gondolas lock their skins like peeling larvae.
The water goes black; the night rises to hunt . . .

Torcello

The green canal, Dutch in its copperplate reserve,
took the rising current of the sea. Seahair lapped
the stone corroded beneath a fingertip arch,

slabs angled for horse and cavalier.
Twined in withered laurel, the hidden Word
spoke to the shrine in the brick wall

shattered by the beatitude of Vermeer.
The grapes were in bud, the pruned stakes
lively with old wounds. In the dark basilica,

under rasps of cloud, the gloomy mosaics burned,
gold tesserae hunted in thick, vengeful image,
flames from the feet of Christ to light the damned.

Their hearty dance woke the antique silence.
The Virgin stood, writhing like a shorn Medusa,
prim with the sexual knowledge of death.

Out in the dusty yard, black-haired girls froze
on marble pedestals, pretending to be Galatea:
stone come to white flesh, come coldly to stone again.

✇ *Venice in February*

> The cattle came upon me with like suddenness,
> staring out of their eyes, and steaming out of
> their nostrils, "Holloa, young thief!"
> —*Great Expectations*

The air grew blunt
with the turmoil of day, gondolas
easing from their slips, dark oars
beating the lagoon to lather,

ragged waves licking the stone.
Flake after flake peeled from a surface
blue as a bruise, pale as the fluttering
vein in an eyelid,

the blue meaning starved of oxygen.
The gilt arabesqued interiors
bloomed, fragile as medusae.
We walked through the renovated palazzo,

where the cracks had already begun to show.
North wind riffled the water,
creased like a bed's newly cold sheets,
the dark ambiguous pleatings of skin

only a lover would know.
The city was almost silent, as if preparing
the nip and tuck of summer's graces,
and yet beneath the silence lay another silence,

indecipherable, transient, your own.

∞ *Leaving Venice*

Blue light across the deserted campo.
Just before dawn, transparent stars
are beached along a worn palazzo.
No, they're painted on! The iron bars

look, in the faint deceits of night,
like a set of false mustaches.
Along the landing, gassy streetlights
flare like a row of matches.

A pride of young policemen stare
at a shop's half-naked mannequins
dressed in the lacy underwear
of the seven deadly sins,

and Venice at this lingering hour
is caught beneath Old World clichés.
We pause below a crumbling tower.
The sky glows like red lingerie

or like a modest local saint.
Above us, large white bras are hung
across the shutters' peeling paint
like warnings in the mother tongue.

Quick! We have to catch our boat!
It lounges at the pier, all sooty-eyed,
as a line of sleepy tourists floats
aboard at low tide.

Two by two, we walk the plank,
swallowed by the consoling dark.
The narrow cabin, still and dank,
smells like Noah's ark.

We cast off onto the black lagoon.
A horn barks once. The motor roars.
St. Theo lifts his rough harpoon
over a city of designer stores.

Now Kenzo and Versace trade
on the streets of ancient slaughter,
where the doges were betrayed
to history's rising water,

and the oily tides will drown
even the sins of history
when Venice in its evening gowns
surrenders to the sea.

The gilt stars rust in the private air.
The sun glints off the public clocks.
We pass a barren island where
men crawl among the naked rocks.

Macbeth in Venice

A little water clears us of this deed.
                                    —*Lady Macbeth*

∾ Prologue

A spiral sun
crossed the spiral stairs.
Each tile, a lost moon
above the café chairs,

glimmered and was gone.
The Adriatic's tears
were given up to pawn
the songs of gondoliers.

And night too was spent
as the campo grew quiet,
having paid its rent
and gone on a diet.

Soon the tide would rise
along the wrinkled canals,
soon the stone revise
gods in their capitals,

the horses of St. Mark's
whinny in their stable,
kick bronze hooves up in sparks,
and slay the sin of Abel,

who chose a martyr's death
and bore the cost of faith
like some unseen Macbeth,
now a broken wraith

who haunts the cold palazzo
crying out the hours
or kneels on fresh terrazzo
in the leaning towers.

Appoint the falling hour
when our ghosts can meet
beneath a winter shower
in Assassin Street.

I. ை *The Witches to the Audience*

Now in your separate stalls, like Circe's pigs,
you wait the transformation of the air,
the phrase's doubtful turn, the word's lost cry,
cold magics reasoned as the falling night
or desperate in their promise as the dawn.
Who stirs the midnight's broth against itself?
Who calls the dinner courses in advance,
each European war, each ship at sea,
or television's retrospective lie?
Take from the grieving map its stormy front,
heir to the rain cloud or pretending sun,
and, where the forecast begs to comprehend
the world's ill future on its coiling winds,
ask who will benefit. The Hanged Man dies
to trump the Visa card; the crystal smog
clears when a gazer has the cash in hand.
O prisoners of fortune, hostages
to each untimely secret seized by us,
you see already what we must predict:
turn to your neighbor, who can name the day
your heart will falter in the cobbled street,
your husband lie, your wife pick up the knife
to stab your sleeping children in their beds.
Each of you knows what someone else suspects,
a secret that could drown a marriage bed,
cut down a hero or erase a sin.
Which of you, silent as the world convicts
some poor dull sap of some real sinner's crime,
would raise a hand if resurrected Christ
were crucified before the shopping mall?
Three robbers died that dusk at Calvary.

Though plays must end, kind evening resurrects
the dying villain from the matinée—
the lovers sip their poison once again;
the husband wads the fatal handkerchief.
On what dark stages will their bartered words
console a disbelieving audience?
We read the future on the dolphin's back,
the secret scrawled upon the watery page
(each woman, man, a wrinkled manuscript),
but in what mirror have we read the past?
Most of you know your life is just an act—
when lovers whisper nothings in your ears,
the phrases part their lips in déjà vu.
Hold your applause. Sit on your shrouded hands
like pairs of wings: these lives must have a life.
Now part the curtain on the black canals.

II. ❦ *Ode to Darkness or,*
The Curtain's Speech

> O our Scots nobles were richt laith
> To weet thir cork-heeled shoon.
> —*Sir Patrick Spens*

Hour of black mist and torches guttering,
    when enemies fall silent in their camp
as figures pass, plotting the death of kings,
    and new guards shuffle through the rising damp;
hour of spent, shallow youth and wasted time,
    hour of fresh traitors and the hopeful cause,
        when the moon scythes ripe shadows overhead,
turning its face to shun the older crime
    of lovers' promises, romantic laws,
        when fleeing owls grip mice between their claws
        and moonlight glimmers on the newly dead.

Who has not heard your footsteps cross
    each discontented park, each haunted stair,
whose architecture of a hidden loss
    consoles the genuflection of the air?
The atmosphere of reason and disgust
    hunts the still campo and the naked street
        your rigid waters cover like the Flood,
sealing each surface in unsleeping rust.
    Now the sad armies as they face defeat,
    now the drowned captain of the sunken fleet,
        will resurrect betrayal in the blood.

Who would have known the muffled night had songs,
    that after blackbirds end their evening round,
still boasting of a life of pretty wrongs,
    the dark erupted in unbroken sound?

In one late choir, night strikes its grieving chord:
  the famous saint lies snoring in his cave,
    a young wolf swaggers toward the bleating sheep,
the mastiff whimpers at the murderer's sword.
  Only the forest creaking on the wave
  reminds the living of the rain⁄soaked grave
    and wakes the darkness to its murdered sleep.

III. &ca; *The Mirror to Lady Macbeth*

I lift my arm, my double lifts hers, too—
tonight we're dressed alike, gold crown, gold shoe.
There's no divide between the *I* and *you.*
    We only do what other lovers do.

Each midnight when we keep this rendezvous
alone, without our noisy retinue,
though I'm alone, I'm not alone with you.
    You only do what other lovers do.

Platonic lovers know they can't be true
divided from each other when they woo,
since if one flees the other can't pursue.
    They only do what other lovers do.

Tell me, my soul, whatever troubles you.
What burdens me will always burden you—
two sisters in one sin, what can we do?
    We only do what other lovers do.

When we were children, every courtier knew
that you were all to me I was to you,
though no one ever said it was taboo.
    You only do what other lovers do.

In long affairs, no stranger has a clue.
Lift your gold robes, just as you always do,
and touch your belly there. I'll do it, too—
    I only do what other lovers do.

Each secret that you whisper *entre nous*
knows love like ours is paid by I.O.U.
Lift your gold dagger—I'll lift mine up, too.
    We only do what other lovers do.

IV. ❧ *The Porter's Song*

True love is not discussed.
Anatomy's unjust:
    a lady's seashell ear
will make a lover lust.
      True love is close to fear—
      Let's drink a little beer.

Though Cupid's barbed harpoon
cannot arrest the moon,
    the octopus and whale
still swim our black lagoon.
      True love was meant to fail—
      Let's drink a little ale.

Law's not the place to start
the murder of the heart.
    The law can't counterfeit her
lies served à la carte.
      True love will not acquit her—
      Let's drink a little bitter.

Climb the rose wall of state
if love has come too late.
    If Hell keeps you in doubt,
love's just a twist of fate.
      True love is not devout—
      Let's drink a little stout.

The shepherd eats the sheep,
but true love makes him weep
    from Lent to Michaelmas
or when he's fast asleep.
      True love is middle-class—
      Let's raise an empty glass.

A porter's what he thinks,
and porter's what he drinks.
        The riddle of the Sphinx?
Love's made of noise and stinks.
        As our fair city sinks,
            true love is draped in minks.

V. &c. *The Murderers' Horses*

Not cold for horses, cold for murderers.
And there we were, three geldings freshly hired
from rotting livery at the Flying Pig.
No one could claim we three were innocents—
our humble inn was off Assassin Street
and we'd been used before, scarred veterans
of moonless missions for the murdered doge.
Old Rackabones had seen the death of kings,
and Whicker tramped a courtesan to death
on orders of some duke. Philosophers
require a thinking mare, milady's maids
the mincing hoof of breeding, state messengers
thick stallions for the whip, the muddy road.
Murderers' horses must be thin, discreet,
able to stare mute hours at underbrush,
not skittish when the snowy night gets bloody.
Beyond the stable door another world
lies glandered, chaotic, the cold hay reeking damp;
within our stalls we know, however cruel
the ostler or the shoes, what to expect:
a horse submits to order—overthrow
the saddle or the bit and knackers reign.
In the dark curve of hell, the glue pot waits.

A king knows bloodstock by its *Sein und Zeit,*
each queen a serviced mare, each heir a foal,
and sires sire their competing stock
across the ruptured borderlands of Europe.
I curry such masters in psychology
and stalk the sinner Abelard in this:
my sin is the intention, not the act.
The devil had a hoof, as kelpies do,
and resurrection of the horse-faced god,

flayed for our sins, demands we chew the bit—
swayback or brood mare, spavined, farcied, lame,
we horses have been reined to suffering.
I saw the play played on the great piazza,
bronze horses of San Marco overhead—
the humpbacked king in battle swore he'd trade
his pocket kingdom for a picket horse.
I, too, suffered castration for my love.

VI. ❧ *Banquo's Feast*

the Cook speaks

Disaster was my favorite recipe.
For dinner I had planned a dozen courses,
each dish prepared as if dead Banquo's soul
now occupied the body of a fowl,
a golden cock Macbeth refused to eat.
Even the linen napkins sailed by water,

though everything in Venice comes by water:
murder or plague, the doctor's recipe
prescribing what a dead man cannot eat.
At first the king demanded fifty courses—
his menu said, *Serve anything but fowl.*
He claimed each chicken had a mortal soul,

that pyrrhic victories scar the feathered soul.
I've seen it on dry land, why not on water?
If souls are animals, why not a fowl,
or singing birds of some strange recipe?
A soul devours a lifetime's worth of courses
in a split second, though it cannot eat.

What does it matter what the victor eats?
Often a victor no longer has a soul,
though he might contemplate religion's courses,
make water wine, turn white wine back to water
(in Venice not a useful recipe).
What's fowl is fare, they say, what's fare is fowl,

though no one cared for seconds of jugged fowl,
or if the soldiers had a scrap to eat,
or how to serve the ghost a recipe.

There *was* a ghost, it's said he had a soul,
though souls are made of nothing more than water.
He disappeared before the final courses.

Now I've refused to cook the king new courses
or ever entertain another fowl.
At dawn I'll leave this tragic port by water
(how else?), bearing aboard raw things to eat.
I want to salvage my immortal soul,
though death has not revealed the recipe.

The water knows the fatal recipe,
the aimless courses of the drowning soul.
I'll leave the circling fowl one thing to eat.

VII. ☙ *Macbeth's Daughter*

A broken mirror is the soul's veneer,
though broken mirrors brought no luck to me.
I'm most impressive when I disappear.

I wander through this drowning atmosphere,
this city built upon a mirrored sea.
A broken mirror is the soul's veneer.

The mute voice is the loveliest, I hear;
but when I speak, there are no words for me.
I'm most persuasive when I disappear.

I took this dagger as a souvenir
and plunged it in the blown glass of the sea.
A broken mirror is the soul's veneer,

and plays are full of daughters—*Hamlet, Lear*—
though most have paid a death to silence me.
I'm most appealing when I disappear.

How could a daughter hope to interfere
against the tidal groaning of the sea?
A broken mirror is the soul's veneer.
I'm most unchanging when I disappear.

VIII. ⚭ *The Guards' Song*

The Queen walks in her sleep
and makes the palace weep.
She'll talk of gates of heaven
at odds of 9–7,

or climb the marble stair
as if dead kings were there.
The odds are 6–5
we'll see the ghosts revive.

> *A soldier bets his lice*
> *against the roll of dice*
> *or quotes the ancient bards*
> *upon a turn of cards.*
> *Though odds run long or short,*
> *true love's the last resort.*

More logical than most
murdered passing ghosts,
she'll spout philosophy
at odds of 8–3.

If murder's sweet intent
requires the grace of Lent,
the odds are 5–6
she'll clutch her crucifix.

> *When battles are discreet,*
> *a soldier gets cold feet;*
> *but, though he can't afford*
> *the dull or rusty sword,*
> *he'd rather pick his nose*
> *than pick the summer rose.*

We'd sooner fight a war
than kiss another whore.
She'll scrub her hands in brine
at odds of 2-9.

Though man contains less blood
than measured by the Flood,
the odds are 1-10
she'll talk of spots again.

> *Whatever's on the face*
> *is not held a disgrace,*
> *though dice are fickle friends*
> *and lovers meet sad ends.*
> *If men are not like gods,*
> *we'd rather play the odds.*

IX. ⮞ *Lady Macbeth on Sleep*

Each shudder takes the mattress by surprise,
though guilt's hard pillow stares you in the face;
the curtains whisper their beguiling lies,
but sleep the soft eraser can't erase.

The night pretends it has no word for me,
I who have walked the corridors in fear
of each new⁄murdered ghost's philosophy,
of acts whose rumor echoes in my ear.

Who when he sleeps is threatened by the real?
The falling ladders seem to comprehend
the fall of states; the nightmare robbers steal
the dagger clenched within the sleeper's hand.

Last night I watched three sisters disagree
on a dead island in the green lagoon;
like Daphne each became a laurel tree
and walked across the black waves streaked with moon.

X. ∞ *Birnam Wood to the Players*

Travel was never one of my desires.
Home takes such mulchy and familiar ground,
a forest won't uproot itself, despite

vacantly longing for a distant coast.
If plants could move, they'd move concealed by night,
shifting the garden to the rose's whim

or rearranging copses in bad taste,
deserting desert countries, crowding the damp,
until each outlaw crop was hunted down.

Only the rootless sneer at having roots:
most oak trees are content just being oaks
and don't feel Daphne got the worst of it.

I don't pretend to love the status quo—
forests grow ignorant of high affairs.
The average tree hears nothing in a wood:

bird song, the snap of twigs, a logger's axe,
the gypsy's Platonist philosophy,
but never a novel or the daily news.

The wind has rumors, like the fleeing deer.
It might be nice to go see for oneself.
In Hades flows a flaming River Sticks

to ferry actors to their last reward.
A myth rewrites a dead philosophy—
from my limbs dropped poor Eve's forbidden fruit,

whose seed has grown the Fortune and the Globe.

What did they eat, the players of the Ark,
when forty nights had drowned the living world

(sloughs, mesas, tundra, fjords, fields of grain)?
Mine were the coiling vines that crawled at dawn;
I stood at noon without a shadow cast;

at dusk I'll walk supported by recruits,
nervous and swearing, one or two in tears.
Each forest knows the riddle of the Sphinx.

Casting three witches or three murderers,
what playwright could be more a silent god
than I? Whether in pencil or blank page,

the history of the stage is carved in wood
(even an actor's said to trod the boards).
A man's not born of woman—he's born of words,

borne down to the grave by words, and words are wood,
from Gutenberg's type case to the humblest sign.
Wood made the Greeks' tarred ships an *Iliad*.

What was the cross? And what the crown of thorns?
One day a forest will convert the Jews.
Though I was the carpenter of each blank verse,

the plotters' friend, the author of the plot,
though each doomed act, each new-laid scene,
was quarreled out beneath my canopy,

I have no need to see Palazzo Dunsinane.
Tonight the slow lagoon is crossed by raft.
The trees of my black wood will be the props.

The trees of my black wood will be the rafts.

XI. ∞ *Macbeth's Daughter Drowned*

I'm most unchanging when I disappear.
A broken mirror is the soul's veneer
against the tidal groaning of the sea.
How could a daughter hope to interfere?

I'm most appealing when I disappear,
though most have paid a death to silence me.
The plays are full of daughters—*Hamlet, Lear*—

but broken mirrors are the soul's veneer
plunged deep into the blown glass of the sea.
I took this dagger as a souvenir.

I'm most persuasive when I disappear,
yet when I speak, there are no words for me.
The mute voice is the loveliest, I hear.

A broken mirror is the soul's veneer,
a city built upon the mirrored sea.
I wander through its drowning atmosphere.

I'm most impressive when I disappear,
though broken mirrors brought no luck to me.
A broken mirror is the soul's veneer.

XII. ◊ *Macbeth the Rationalist*

When Birnam Wood sets sail for Dunsinane,
the play must end. All the scarred props of state,
the doomed palazzo fortified in vain,

become a history of the second rate.
Beginnings are the incarnated end
of every fairy tale, whose duplicate

mirror, reflection, twin, or bosom friend
says nothing ever happens less than twice.
Though Vico knew our histories descend

circle by circle into Dante's ice,
the dampest cellar of original sin
does not pretend old virtue has no vice—

the only quarrel's whether gold or tin
will satisfy the God on Heaven's throne
(though some suspect He takes His glass of gin).

Save us from gods who love themselves alone,
who need the burr of beatific love
bleated by angels in pale baritone

or cooed each morning by the mourning dove.
Our fallen world loves malice on the air;
the cold assassin wears a velvet glove

to mop his brow, or part his victim's hair.
A king buys murder on installment plan
to stab a rival, suffocate an heir,

or justify the ways of God to man
by firm example. Though the have-nots shiver
when kings do what immortal beings can,

twice entering old Heraclitus' river,
we want a king of intellect and reason,
whose oracles consult his beak-torn liver,

a proud Prometheus for every season.
Having assassinated kind King Log,
though no one would consider it real treason,

King Stork has ordered supper by the bog,
a king in appetite, ready to dine
on every equal citizen and frog.

A king inherits the Darwinian line.

LONDON, 1606

I should address you as my master, not
an equal prince astride an equal state.
How well my Venice grips her liberty.
The Jesuit sedition was a spark
to light the sleeping powder keg of Europe,
that dreaming realm that coils now between us,
a greasy eel muscled with avarice.
The virgin dust was ripe with Jesuits;
the gleam on windows took the Jesuit gleam;
the downing sun, the risen moon, each spoke
in phrases Jesuit priests could conjugate.
Let none embark upon your isolate islands,
whose rivers have been tamed to smooth canals,
whose palaces afloat on timber rafts
glow with spent chandeliers in dank lagoons,
their windows faceted like shattered mirrors,
each living beam a peaceful remonstrance
to hooded creatures chanting in the mire.
The universe declines the right of man
by just necessity, as scripture shows—
the Fall of Rome, the Flood, the apple torn
from branches on the tree in Paradise,
were each the hidden work of Jesuits.
The furious plague that tortured London came
in Jesuit purses wrapped in holy cloths;
and here my gilded House of Parliament
above the mirrored surface of the Thames
was taken almost to the gate of Doom
by Jesuit conspirators, their hands
stretched in unholy midnight ritual

to light the fuse of a gunpowder plot.
The speechless earth an inch from dire combustion
forgot their purposes—and we were spared.
The Serenissima cannot afford
the candles of such worship on its streets.
My island is a melon, let it speak
in fondness to your grape-sized pocket realm,
island to island, king to doge, as if
we walked the corridors of Hampton Palace.
A merchant prince should know what merchants are—
shall our own words bring nought? Here we have seen
the chambered priest, the hiding hole that stops
new dough from rising at the hearth, the prayer
wasping away in chimney smoke, the babe
bawling its cataracts out to believe.
Equivocation is the Jesuit God
until the words of our own Bible breed
loyal translations for disloyal times.
Knowing you loathe the odor of Jesuits,
I send you by this hand, to mark the fate
of those who kill a king, a play on traitors.
Their God would turn His other cheek to lie,
and Father Garnet has confirmed His lie
in sweat-soaked perjury upon the gallows.
So lately have we dealt with traitors here.

∞ *Notes*

Punchinello in Chains: In his late age, the Venetian artist Domenico Tiepolo (1727–1804) took to drawing invented scenes from the life of the commedia dell'arte character Punchinello, who wore a beaklike mask and conical hat. Tiepolo completed a hundred or more drawings, sometimes of fantastic character. There is an implied narrative, but confused, incomplete, or purposely misleading. The album containing the grotesque humane comedy of Punchinello survived intact until 1921, when it was broken up and sold.

Macbeth in Venice: For reasons of state diplomacy, shortly after the Gunpowder Plot and the expulsion of Jesuits from Venice, James VI and I sent an altered version of *Macbeth* to the doge.

❧ Biographical Note

William Logan lives in Florida and in Cambridge, England.

⮂ Penguin Poets

TED BERRIGAN
Selected Poems
The Sonnets

PHILIP BOOTH
Lifelines

JIM CARROLL
Fear of Dreaming
Void of Course

CARL DENNIS
Practical Gods

DIANE DI PRIMA
Loba

STUART DISCHELL
Dig Safe

STEPHEN DOBYNS
Pallbearers Envying the
* One Who Rides*
The Porcupine's Kisses

ROGER FANNING
Homesick

AMY GERSTLER
Crown of Weeds
Medicine
Nerve Storm

DEBORA GREGER
Desert Fathers, Uranium
* Daughters*
God

ROBERT HUNTER
Sentinel

BARBARA JORDAN
Trace Elements

MARY KARR
Viper Rum

JACK KEROUAC
Book of Blues
Book of Haikus

JOANNE KYGER
As Ever

ANN LAUTERBACH
If in Time
On a Stair

PHYLLIS LEVIN
Mercury

WILLIAM LOGAN
Macbeth in Venice
Night Battle
Vain Empires

DEREK MAHON
Selected Poems

MICHAEL MCCLURE
Huge Dreams:
* San Francisco and*
* Beat Poems*

CAROL MUSKE
An Octave Above
* Thunder*

ALICE NOTLEY
The Descent of Alette
Disobedience
Mysteries of Small
* Houses*

LAWRENCE RAAB
The Probable World
Visible Signs

STEPHANIE
STRICKLAND
V

ANNE WALDMAN
Kill or Cure
Marriage: A Sentence

PHILIP WHALEN
Overtime: Selected
* Poems*

ROBERT WRIGLEY
Reign of Snakes

JOHN YAU
Borrowed Love Poems